MARY HOFFMAN has written over a hundred books for children that range from picture books to teenage fiction. *Amazing Grace* celebrated its twenty-fifth anniversary in 2016 and has become a modern classic. Mary's Great Big Book series, illustrated by Ros Asquith, is available in eighteen countries and *The Great Big Book of Families* won the SLA Information Book Award. You can find out more about Mary and her books at: www.maryhoffman.co.uk

ROS ASQUITH has been a *Guardian* cartoonist for 20 years, and has written and illustrated over 70 books for young people, including the bestseller *The Great Big Book of Families*, with Mary Hoffman, the Teenage Worrier series, *Letters from an Alien Schoolboy* – which was shortlisted for the Roald Dahl Funny Prize – her debut picture story book *It's Not Fairy* and her poetry collection *Vanishing Trick*. For more information about Ros, visit her website: www.rosasquith.co.uk

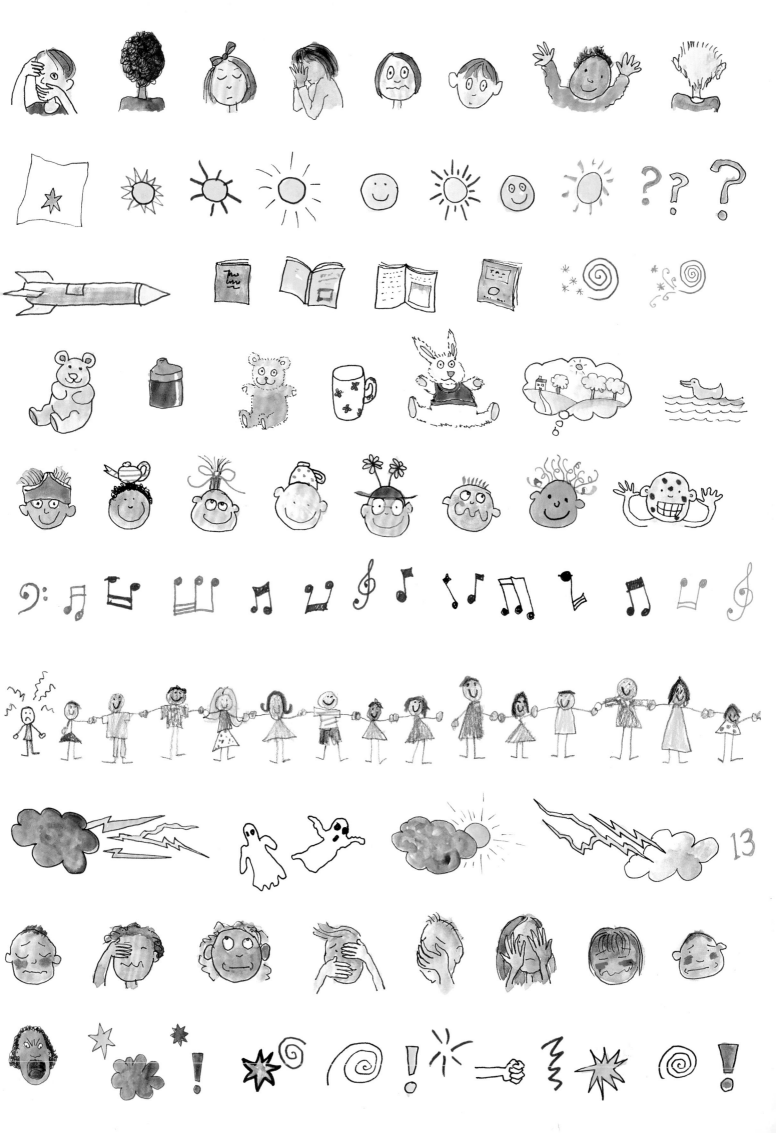

For Viola and Elodie Harvey, with love - MH
To Isabel, Alexina and Charlotte, with love - RA

Q Quarto Knows

JANETTA OTTER-BARRY BOOKS

The Great Big Book of Feelings copyright © Frances Lincoln Limited 2013
Text copyright © Mary Hoffman 2013
Illustrations copyright © Ros Asquith 2013

First published in Great Britain and in the USA in 2013 by
Frances Lincoln Children's Books, 74-77 White Lion Street, London N1 9PF
QuartoKnows.com
Visit our blogs at QuartoKnows.com

This first paperback edition published in 2016

A catalogue record for this book is available from the British Library.

ISBN 978-1-84780-758-8

Illustrated with watercolours

Set in Green

Printed in China

1 3 5 7 9 8 6 4 2

MIX
Paper from
responsible sources
FSC® C104723
FSC
www.fsc.org

# The Great Big Book of Feelings

Can you find ME every time you turn a page?

**Mary Hoffman**

**Illustrated by Ros Asquith**

Frances Lincoln
Children's Books

# How do you feel today?

How do you think these children are feeling?

It isn't always easy to tell.

# HAPPY

What makes you happy?

Very nice. Now, where's my supper?

Perhaps cuddling your pet.

Or reading your favourite book.

Some people just seem born happier than others.

And it can be enough for the sun to be shining to make you feel very happy.

A rainy day can make you sad. But that's a small sadness.

Sorry, I forgot

Someone forgetting it's your birthday is a bigger one.

But when someone you love dies the sadness feels so big it covers all your life – like the biggest rain cloud ever.

RIP

# EXCITED

What makes you feel excited?

We can get very excited just about going on an outing.

But some people do *really* exciting things like jumping out of planes or climbing high mountains.

What's the most exciting thing you've ever done?

# Bored

When there is nothing exciting going on, you can feel bored. Grown-ups hate it when you say "I'm bored". Maybe because they never have time to be bored.

Something you think is boring might turn out to be interesting – even exciting – if you give it a try!

# ANGRY

**What makes you angry?**

**OUCH!**

Little things like stubbing your toe?
Or when parents or teachers are being unfair?

A horrible hot feeling bubbles up
inside you and you want to shout
at someone or throw things.

Often we take out our angry feelings
on people – or things! – just because
they are there.

Hisssss

cats wag
their tails
when
they're
angry

What can you do when you feel angry, instead of hurting other people?

Count to ten.

Go for a walk.

Shout.

Do an angry dance.

Draw an angry picture.

Stamp.

Punch an angry cushion.

Sometimes feeling angry can be good.

KIDS NEED BOOKS

SAVE OUR LIBRARY

# UPSET

Some things would make anyone upset!

Being ignored by your friends. . .

being bullied. . . or losing someone you love. . . you'd have to be a robot not to be upset by things like these.

But some people find it upsetting to move house or go to a new school, while others see those times as exciting.

**Calm**

What do you do to calm down after you've been upset?

Some people feel calm when they are near water, because of the soothing sound.

Whatever makes you feel calm and peaceful might be a good thing to think about when you feel upset.

Sometimes you just feel in a silly mood.

You might want to do or say or be something very silly.

SILLY CAFE

Jumping Beans
Roast Beef and Custard
Apple pie with Ketchup
Frog-in-a-basket

Even grown-ups get this feeling sometimes.

# L.NELY

Everyone feels lonely
sometimes.

Maybe it's because
you feel you haven't
got any friends. Or you
think you are different
from everyone else in
the world.

Sometimes you can feel very lonely
even in the middle of a crowd of people.
Especially if you have just arrived
to live in a new country.

I know she won't be my friend...

The best way to make friends is to be friendly yourself. You never know – maybe other people are feeling lonely too!

# SCARED

What scares you? People can be scared of all sorts of things – spiders, heights, dogs, saying their name out loud, the dark, snakes, the number 13.

Some people are even scared of knees!

But mostly we are scared because we are afraid someone or something will hurt us or someone close to us.

BANG!

CRASH!

# SAFE

What makes you feel safe and not scared at all?

Perhaps being indoors in the warm when it's dark and cold outside?

Snuggling under the covers at bedtime? Having someone to look after you that you trust?

**Embarrassed**

Have you ever felt really embarrassed? We all have embarrassing moments that make us want to hide when we think of them!

Maybe one of your parents has embarrassed you in public?

Jack! You've forgotten your TEDDY!

SCHOOL TRIP

Nobody likes being made to look a fool in front of other people, but it happens to all of us.

Some people don't seem to mind though – they never feel embarrassed.

**Shy**

Are you a shy person?
Most people feel shy
sometimes but some of
us feel shy all the time.

If you don't like meeting new people, or
don't like saying anything in a big group,
or if you hide behind your hair or a book,
you are probably a shy person!

Why's she wearing
a pillow case?
Did she think it
was fancy dress?

No. She's
just shy.

Other people seem really confident all the time. But you can bet some of them are feeling really shy inside.

I know the answer but I'm too shy to say.

 MY BROTHER IS ILL

 WORRIED

Bullies

What sort of things do you worry about?

Grown-ups worry about big things like money and if your parents argue in front of you, that can be worrying for you too.

What do you do when you feel worried? The best thing to do is tell someone how you are feeling.

 DAD IS SAD

 something bad happening

There's a Swedish proverb that says "worry often gives a small thing a big shadow".

But if there's no one you can tell, you can write down everything you are worried about.

Jealousy is a really horrible feeling! It can come when you think a person likes someone else more than they like you. You might feel jealous of a brother or sister.

You can even feel jealous of a friend.

It's one of the hardest feelings to get rid of but it's good to learn not to be jealous if you can.

All the other cats have got their supper

Some people call jealousy "the green-eyed monster".

How to destroy green eyed MONSTER

~~Shooting poison~~
Find new friends.
Make life more FAIR! ✓

Perhaps you can think of ways to destroy the monster of feeling jealous?

# SATISFIED

Do you remember what it was like before you could stand or walk? Probably not! But when babies and small children are learning to do something, they just keep on trying until they get it right.

You want that shiny object that's just out of reach so you stretch tall to get it.

BIG DIPPER

→

YOU MUST BE THIS HEIGHT TO RIDE

10/10 A+

10/10 A*

Hah! Eight months older than me and still not walking

But isn't it a satisfying feeling when you do manage
to complete the task or get the thing you wanted?

Piano Grade 1

CYCLING PROFICIENCY

I CAN HOP

I CAN READ

# FEELING BETTER

Some people think that feelings are private and shouldn't be talked about. Others say it's good to let people know how you feel – then maybe something can be done to help you feel better when you feel bad.

Sharing a good feeling might make someone else feel better.

There are lots more ways of feeling than in this book –
see how many you can think of.

And you can feel lots
of different things at
the same time.
Or lots of different
ways in one day.

How are
YOU
feeling
now?

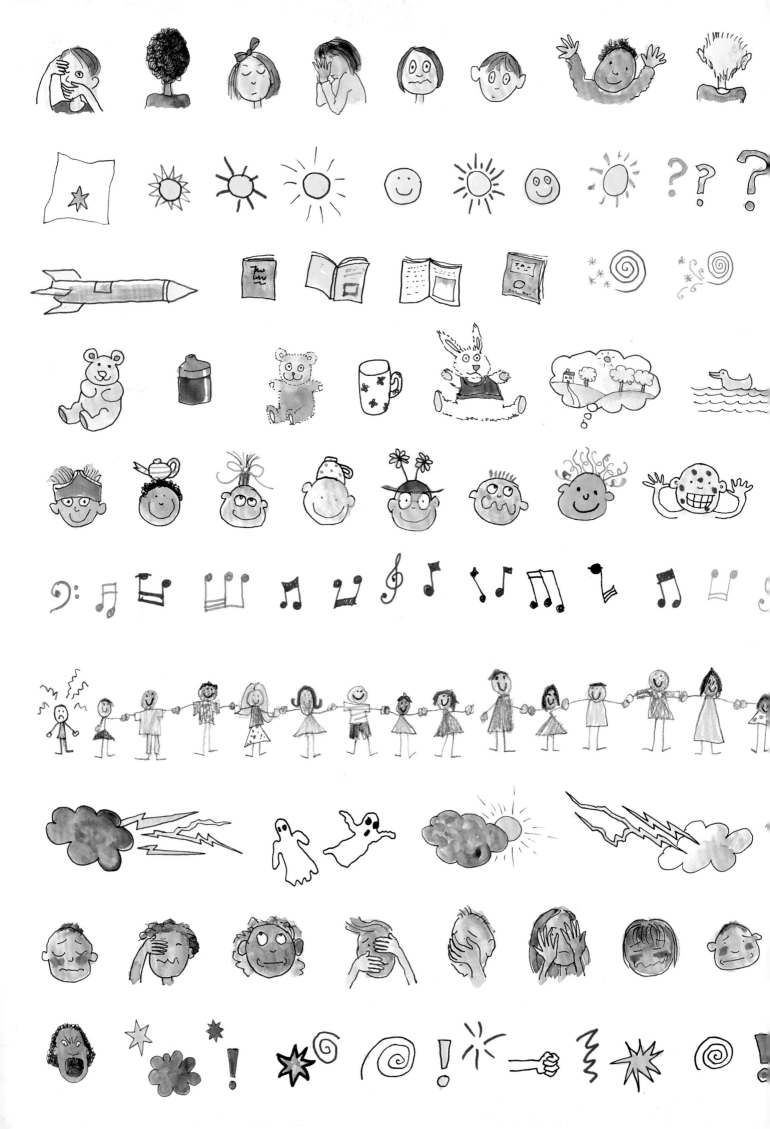

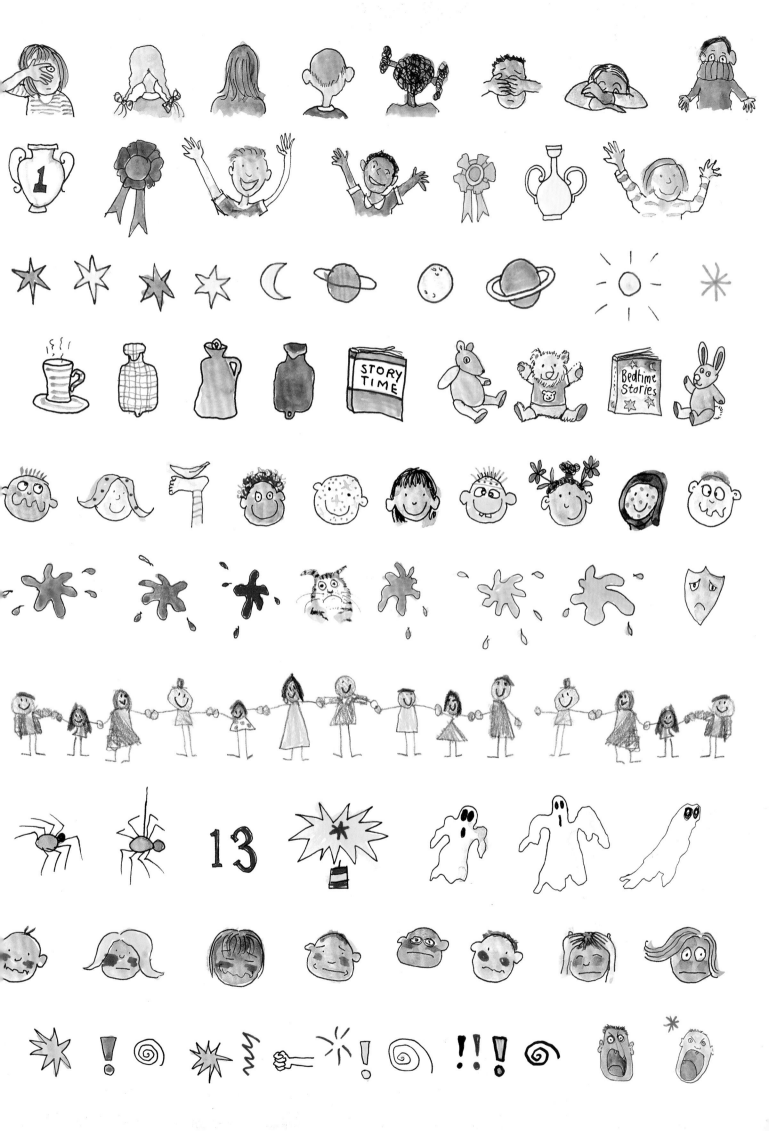

# MORE TITLES BY MARY HOFFMAN AND ROS ASQUITH
# FROM FRANCES LINCOLN CHILDREN'S BOOKS

### The Great Big Book of Families
by Mary Hoffman and Ros Asquith
978-1-84780-587-4

What is a family? Once, it was said to be a father, mother, boy, girl, cat and dog living in a house with a garden. But as times have changed, families have changed too, and now there are almost as many kinds of families as colours of the rainbow, from a mum and dad to single parent or two mums or two dads, from a mixed-race family to different mums and dads. What is your family like?

Winner of the SLA Information Book Award
"A sublimely simple idea, brilliantly executed." — *Kirkus*

### The Great Big Green Book
by Mary Hoffman and Ros Asquith
978-1-84780-445-7

Do you care about saving endangered animals, protecting our precious forests and plants, keeping our air, oceans and fresh water clean and safe? Find out all the things you can do to help – turn off taps, make compost, grow plants for bees, ask questions. Keep our planet safe and GREEN for the children of the future. Your planet needs YOU!

'An inspiring guide with hope for the future of our planet'
— *Books for Keeps*

### Welcome to the Family
by Mary Hoffman and Ros Asquith
978-1-84780-461-7

How did you arrive in your family? Have you got a mum and dad, or a step-mum, or foster parents, or maybe two dads, or two mums? Find out about the many different ways of making a family. Maybe you can find one like yours!

"A wonderfully inclusive look at all the ways children can become part of a family. A really important and accessible information book for younger children." — *The Bookseller*

Shortlisted for the SLA Information Book Award

Frances Lincoln titles are available from all good bookshops.
You can also buy books and find out more about your favourite titles,
authors and illustrators on our website: www.franceslincoln.com